MW01296840

"The Gr
'Living by Grace through Faith'
By David M. Gillespie

*This and other titles by David M. Gillespie are
also available
For your Kindle app or device.
Go to: http://amazon.com/author/davidmgillespie*
You may contact David directly via e-mail:
david@davidmgillespie.com

"The Greatest Thing"
'Living by Grace through Faith'
By David M. Gillespie

Table of Contents:

Foreword

In November 1964, at the age of eight years, in a little Baptist Church in Diamond, West Virginia, I made Jesus Christ the Lord of my life. I believe my life is a monument to the grace and mercy of God. I have experienced firsthand, His mercy and compassion, His forgiveness, His restoring, blessing and miraculous healing power. I can tell you by experience that God never fails. More importantly, it is the Holy Bible, which is God's Word that tells us He never fails. It tells us that God NEVER changes. He is always faithful and His promises are true. It is the Bible – God's Word and His Word alone, upon which I base my faith and my teaching.

I have always enjoyed watching sports. One of my earliest memories of sports on television is seeing the camera zoom in on the edge of the field to show a person holding up a big white poster with John 3:16 written in big letters: Of course John 3:16 says, "For God so loved the world that He gave His only begotten son that whosoever believeth on Him should not perish but have everlasting life." It is one of the most memorized and frequently quoted verses of Scripture. In this one little verse, Jesus tells us the greatest thing about God, the greatest thing that God ever did and the greatest thing that ever happened to each and every member of the human race. That GREATEST thing is the subject of this book.

I am excited to share this teaching with you. I sincerely pray and believe that the Holy Spirit, the Teacher of the church, will increase our knowledge of Him and that He will reveal to us, the great, everlasting love of our Lord Jesus Christ so that we will be filled with all the fullness of God.

Chapter 1
"The Greatest Thing about God"

John 3:16 For God so loved the world, that he gave his only begotten Son, that whosoever believeth in him should not perish, but have everlasting life.

If you walk up to a stranger on the street and ask them if they believe in God, you will get all sorts of answers. Some people will tell you they don't believe in God. Other people may tell you what they think of the church where they grew up. Some people may tell you they believe in God…BUT. Then others will say of course they believe, praise God and you have met a fellow believer. However, all of those people – even ones who claim to not believe in God or any supreme being, will, almost without exception, tell you that if there is a God, He must be all powerful. If there is a God, that God would have to be almighty. Of course, the Bible does teach us that God is almighty. In the Book of Genesis, He introduced Himself to Abram by saying, "I am Almighty God". Throughout the pages of the bible, God is described as capable of things that the human mind cannot explain or even accept happening. Here is a passage of Scripture in Isaiah that tells us a bit about the greatness of God:

Isaiah 40:21Haven't you heard? Don't you understand?
Are you deaf to the words of God—

the words he gave before the world began?
   Are you so ignorant?
22 God sits above the circle of the earth.
   The people below seem like grasshoppers to him!
He spreads out the heavens like a curtain
   and makes his tent from them.
23 He judges the great people of the world
   and brings them all to nothing.
24 They hardly get started, barely taking root,
   when he blows on them and they wither.
   The wind carries them off like chaff.
25 "To whom will you compare me?
   Who is my equal?" asks the Holy One.
26 Look up into the heavens.
   Who created all the stars?
He brings them out like an army, one after another,
   calling each by its name.
Because of his great power and incomparable strength,
   not a single one is missing
(NLT)

God draws the heavens out like a curtain. He created the stars and calls each one by name. A famous astronomer who passed away several years ago, was famous for saying that there are "billions and billions" of stars. Verse 22 says that God sits on the circle of the earth. It is said about Christopher Columbus that he learned by reading the Bible that the earth isn't flat. The scientific leaders of his day believed the earth was flat and that if a ship went too far out to sea, it would simply drop off the edge. Columbus saw that God sits on the CIRCLE of the earth. Because he believed the Bible, he went out and saw what was on the other side of that circle.

Genesis 1:1 In the beginning God created the heaven and the earth.

2 And the earth was without form, and void; and darkness was upon the face of the deep. And the Spirit of God moved upon the face of the waters.

3 And God said, Let there be light: and there was light.

There is a line of scientific thought that explains the origin of the universe by what is called the "Big Bang Theory". It basically says that there was a point of time in the vast eons of the past when all at once, an explosion took place and particles spun off into the void and eventually settled into galaxies and solar systems and finally the worlds as we now know them. Most astronomers of whom I am aware, agree that the universe is expanding at 186,000 miles per second. That is the speed of light. Albert Einstein wrote on a chalk board, the equation, E=MCsq. That means energy (E) equals matter (M) by the speed of light, squared (C). He saw that the relation between energy and matter is a point of acceleration related to the speed of light. God said "Let there be light". Light was. That light energy was the spiritual material the Holy Spirit used to craft this natural universe, so that things which are seen were not made of nothing, but made of that which was not seen (Hebrews 12:3). It has taken scientists a long time to start to catch up with the God who created science. I am convinced as surely as I'm convinced that this morning, the sun rose in the east, that the more we truly understand science and the more we truly understand the Bible, the more we will see total agreement. There was another well known, celebrated scientist who said that he is searching for a "single theory". He is looking for a single thing that will explain EVERYTHING. I can help this scientist. Genesis 1:1 says "In the beginning, GOD..." That's the single theory that he seeks, but it's not a theory. It's the Word of God.

Some time ago, my wife and I went on a missions trip to Bogota, Colombia. We were approached by a young lady who said that she has friends who say they don't believe in God. She asked me what she could say to them to help them see that God is real. I am a visual artist. God has blessed me with the opportunity to create works of art at many public events and to see my work displayed around the world. I told this to the young lady and asked her this question: Where does creativity come from? You see, creativity is born in the heart of every human. That's what Picasso and others have been quoted as saying - that every child is born an artist – the challenge is remaining an artist after one grows up. That's why restaurants have crayons and a coloring sheet with their kids' menu. Place any small child at a table with paper and crayon and they are going to create something. It's just natural. Some people go astray and don't seem creative but creativity is born in us. Humans are creators. Trees make other trees. Bees make other bees. Birds make other birds. Grass and flowers produce more grass and flowers.

Genesis 1:26 And God said, Let us make man in our image, after our likeness: and let them have dominion over the fish of the sea, and over the fowl of the air, and over the cattle, and over all the earth, and over every creeping thing that creepeth upon the earth.

27 So God created man in his own image, in the image of God created he him; male and female created he them.

Everything produces after its kind. People are natural creators because the Creator Himself made us in His very image - of the Creator. We can't eat an oil painting. A drawing of a flower has absolutely nothing to do with the survival of our species. We create because our Heavenly Father created us to be like Him. That's how I explained it to the young lady in Bogota. We are exhibit "A" on the list of irrefutable evidence that God exists and that He created the universe.

The Bible tells us that God is omnipotent, or ALL powerful:

Revelation 1:8 I am Alpha and Omega, the beginning and the ending, saith the Lord, which

is, and which was, and which is to come, the Almighty.

The Bible tells us that God is omniscient, or ALL knowing:

Job 29:24 For He looks to the ends of the earth and sees everything under the heavens.
(AMP)

The Bible tells us that God is omni – present or that He is EVERYWHERE:

Jeremiah 23:24 Can any hide himself in secret places that I shall not see him? saith the LORD. Do not I fill heaven and earth? saith the LORD.

The Bible gives us great, glorious descriptions of God that leave no doubt that God is all powerful, all knowing, and ever present. In Psalm 139, we see all of these attributes described in poetic praise to Him:

Psalm 139:1 O LORD, You have searched me and known *me.*
2 You know my sitting down and my rising up; You understand my thought afar off.
3 You comprehend my path and my lying down, And are acquainted with all my ways.
4 For *there is* not a word on my tongue, *But* behold, O LORD, You know it altogether.
5 You have hedged me behind and before, And laid Your hand upon me.
6 *Such* knowledge *is* too wonderful for me; It is high, I cannot *attain* it.
7 Where can I go from Your Spirit? Or where can I flee from Your presence?

8 If I ascend into heaven, You *are* there;
If I make my bed in hell, behold, You *are there.*
9 *If* I take the wings of the morning,
And dwell in the uttermost parts of the sea,
10 Even there Your hand shall lead me,
And Your right hand shall hold me.
11 If I say, "Surely the darkness shall fall on me,"
Even the night shall be light about me;
12 Indeed, the darkness shall not hide from You,
But the night shines as the day;
The darkness and the light *are* both alike *to You.*
13 For You formed my inward parts;
You covered me in my mother's womb.
14 I will praise You, for I am fearfully *and* wonderfully made;
Marvelous are Your works,
And *that* my soul knows very well.
(NKJV)

The last verse says "Marvelous are Your works and that my soul knows very well." The soul of man is his mind. Our minds are well aware of God's marvelous works. What is "marvelous"? It's a marvel. It's something spectacular. Do you see all this around you? Look at some internet videos of what is under the surface of the ocean and the vast reaches of outer space. God is awesome. He is great beyond human comprehension. God's creation is spectacular –

marvelous! Yet this is not the greatest thing about God. What is the greatest thing about God? Why did He create the universe? Why did He make you? Our main verse of Scripture, John 3:16 tells us. It says, "For God so loved".

1 John 4:8 Anyone who does not love does not know God, for God is love.
(MEV)

THIS is the greatest thing about God. He has all power and His presence fills the whole universe. He knows everything. But He IS love. He is perfect, patient, unselfish, lavishly generous, understanding, tender, merciful, compassionate love. Why did He create the universe? God is love. Why did He make you? God is love. Why did He Give His only begotten Son to die on a cross? God IS love. THIS is the greatest thing about God.

Chapter 2
"The Greatest Thing God Ever Did"

John 3:16 For God so loved the world, that he gave his only begotten Son, that whosoever believeth in him should not perish, but have everlasting life.

Our beginning verse not only tells us the greatest thing about God but it tells us the greatest thing that God ever did. We have talked about the vast wonderful creation of the universe. Everything that is seen was made of God's Word – spoken into existence. But that isn't the greatest thing God ever did. John 3:16 says that God SO loved the world that He GAVE His only begotten Son. This Son is Jesus Christ. God the Father didn't merely send Jesus to earth to give us a greeting, or a message, or to see how people would react to Him. Jesus Christ is the Son of God. He was sent. He was given. He was given up to die in our place. The Bible tells us that unto us, a child was born and unto us a SON was given!

Isaiah 9:6 For unto us a child is born, unto us a son is given: and the government shall be upon his shoulder: and his name shall be called Wonderful, Counsellor, The mighty God, The everlasting Father, The Prince of Peace.

Unto us a child is born and a son is given. God the Father loved you and me so much that He gave His only begotten son to take upon Himself the punishment for all the sin of mankind –

including yours and mine. The sending of Jesus, wrapped up in who He is and what He came to do, is the greatest thing that God ever did. Look at the setting of John 3:16. So often, we read it and quote it just because it's such a wonderful verse of Scripture with such an extravagant meaning. This took place at night, when a very important man came privately to talk with Jesus.

John 3:1, 2 After dark one night a Jewish religious leader named Nicodemus, a member of the sect of the Pharisees, came for an interview with Jesus. "Sir," he said, "we all know that God has sent you to teach us. Your miracles are proof enough of this."

3 Jesus replied, "With all the earnestness I possess I tell you this: Unless you are born again, you can never get into the Kingdom of God."

(TLB)

Nicodemus had a very special religious education. He was a very important man among the Jewish people. Jesus told Him the spiritual key to the whole story – Man must be born again. Later on in this book, we will look more deeply into what that means but this is the setting for our story. Jesus was not on top of a mountain, proclaiming a message to a multitude. He was explaining to Nicodemus what the world really needed, how it was going to be made available and the central role that Jesus had in making it happen. Look at what Jesus said just prior to the 16th verse:

John 3:14 And as Moses lifted up the serpent in the wilderness, even so must the Son of man be lifted up:
15 That whosoever believeth in him should not perish, but have eternal life.

Jesus points to an incident that took place after the people of Israel had been led out of Egypt but had not yet entered the Promised Land. The people had fallen into sin and provoked the wrath of God. Snakes went into the camp and bit the people and people were dying. Moses prayed for the people and God gave a plan to save the ones who had been bitten. There is a lot of symbolism in this story, as many things that happened in the Old Testament are symbolic, pointing to what would come about through Jesus and everything He did.

Numbers 21:4 Then the people of Israel set out from Mount Hor, taking the road to the Red Sea to go around the land of Edom. But the people grew impatient with the long journey,
5 And they began to speak against God and Moses. "Why have you brought us out of Egypt to die here in the wilderness?" they complained. "There is nothing to eat here and nothing to drink. And we hate this horrible manna!"
6 So the LORD sent poisonous snakes among the people, and many were bitten and died.
7 Then the people came to Moses and cried out, "We have sinned by speaking against the LORD and against you. Pray that the LORD will take

away the snakes." So Moses prayed for the people.

8 Then the LORD **told him, "Make a replica of a poisonous snake and attach it to a pole. All who are bitten will live if they simply look at it!"**

9 So Moses made a snake out of bronze and attached it to a pole. Then anyone who was bitten by a snake could look at the bronze snake and be healed!

(NLT)

This is the scene to which Jesus referred when talking to Nicodemus that night. Obviously speaking of His coming crucifixion, He said that as Moses lifted up the serpent in the wilderness, He must also be lifted up. The people had sinned and the penalty of that sin was death by serpent. To cure the bite of the serpent, a brass image was to be lifted up. Whoever looked to that brass figure of a serpent on a pole would live. But God gave His only begotten Son. Jesus is the perfect sacrifice for all time for our sin, the "Lamb slain from the foundation of the world" (Revelation 13:8) why wasn't that a lamb on the pole, if it's a symbol of Jesus? It's not merely a symbol of Him. It's a symbol of what He did. Since the Garden of Eden, the serpent was used as a symbol of the devil. In Luke 10:19, Jesus said He gives us authority to tread on "serpents and scorpions and over all the power of the enemy and nothing shall by any means hurt you." This episode in the wilderness showed death as the penalty for sin, just as God told Adam and Eve in the Garden, if they disobeyed Him, they would die. That is what happened. Their sin separated them from God. It put mankind into the terrible state of spiritual death – separation from God and His blessing. A curse came on the earth and man was under the dominion of an outlaw spirit named Satan. The brass serpent on that pole was an image of Satan. Bible scholars without exception agree that brass is used in the Bible to represent judgment.

John 16:7 Nevertheless I tell you the truth; It is expedient for you that I go away: for if I go not away, the Comforter will not come unto you; but if I depart, I will send him unto you.
8 And when he is come, he will reprove the world of sin, and of righteousness, and of judgment:
9 Of sin, because they believe not on me;
10 Of righteousness, because I go to my Father, and ye see me no more;
11 Of judgment, because the prince of this world is judged.

Look at verse 11. The prince of this world is judged. That brass serpent represented judgment of Satan and everything he represents and everything he did in the fall of Adam. Jesus carried it up on that cross. The serpent on the pole represents the end of Satan's dominion over man! That's what Jesus did!

1 John 3:8 [But] he who commits sin [who practices evildoing] is of the devil [takes his

character from the evil one], for the devil has sinned (violated the divine law) from the beginning. The reason the Son of God was made manifest (visible) was to undo (destroy, loosen, and dissolve) the works the devil [has done].

Jesus told Nicodemus that He would be lifted up just like that serpent. Just as everyone who looked at that brass serpent on the pole was saved from death, whosoever believes on Jesus will not perish but have everlasting life. God loved us so much that He gave His Son to suffer in our place. Jesus died in our place and was raised from the dead.

Ephesians 1:17 That the God of our Lord Jesus Christ, the Father of glory, may give unto you the spirit of wisdom and revelation in the knowledge of him:

18 The eyes of your understanding being enlightened; that ye may know what is the hope of his calling, and what the riches of the glory of his inheritance in the saints,

19 And what is the exceeding greatness of his power to us-ward who believe, according to the working of his mighty power,

20 Which he wrought in Christ, when he raised him from the dead, and set him at his own right hand in the heavenly places,

21 Far above all principality, and power, and might, and dominion, and every name that is named, not only in this world, but also in that which is to come:

22 And hath put all things under his feet, and gave him to be the head over all things to the church,
23 Which is his body, the fulness of him that filleth all in all.

In the first and third chapters of Paul's letter to the Ephesians, he prays Holy Spirit inspired prayers for the church. We would do well to pray each of these prayers for ourselves and for fellow believers. In verse 19 above, Paul prays that God would open our spiritual eyes so that we would know the exceeding greatness of God's power. Not the power of God in the creation of the world, that we read about in Chapter one, but the exceeding greatness of His power that He used when He raised Jesus from the dead and seated Him at His own right hand (The seat of authority) FAR ABOVE the devil and all his forces. The greatest expression of God's love is what motivated the greatest expression of His power!

Colossians 2:11 When you came to Christ, you were "circumcised," but not by a physical procedure. Christ performed a spiritual circumcision—the cutting away of your sinful nature.   12 For you were buried with Christ when you were baptized. And with him you were raised to new life because you trusted the mighty power of God, who raised Christ from the dead.
13 You were dead because of your sins and because your sinful nature was not yet cut

away. Then God made you alive with Christ, for he forgave all our sins.

14 He canceled the record of the charges against us and took it away by nailing it to the   15 In this way, he disarmed the spiritual rulers and authorities. He shamed them publicly by his victory over them on the cross.
(NLT)

Jesus disarmed Satan and all his spiritual cohorts. He shamed them publicly and cancelled out the charges that were against us because of sin. When Adam and Eve sinned, they were separated from God. They died spiritually and Satan gained dominion over them. Through this spiritually dead condition, Satan ruled over all mankind until Jesus was sacrificed in our place and then raised up.

Romans 5: 18, 19 Here it is in a nutshell: Just as one person did it wrong and got us in all this trouble with sin and death, another person did it right and got us out of it. But more than just getting us out of trouble, he got us into life! One man said no to God and put many people in the wrong; one man said yes to God and put many in the right.
(MSG)

God sent the perfect sacrifice to pay for the sin of all mankind and not only took away our sin but raised Jesus from the dead and completely stripped the devil of his dominion over man. THIS is the greatest thing that God ever did!

Chapter 3
"The Greatest Thing that Ever Happened to You"

John 3:16 For God so loved the world, that he gave his only begotten Son, that whosoever believeth in him should not perish, but have everlasting life.

We know the greatest thing about God and the greatest thing that God ever did. Love Himself gave the best that He had. Jesus Christ and everything He did on earth, under the earth and in Heaven above, is motivated by God's great love. But what does that really mean to each one of us as individuals? Our main verse of Scripture also tells us the greatest thing that ever happened to you. "Whosoever believes on Jesus should not perish but have everlasting life". The Amplified Bible makes it very clear:

John 3:16 For God so greatly loved *and* dearly prized the world that He [even] gave up His only begotten (unique) Son, so that whoever believes in (trusts in, clings to, relies on) Him shall not perish (come to destruction, be lost) but have eternal (everlasting) life.
(AMP)

Keep in mind that when you see in the Bible, the word "whosoever" or "whoever", it's speaking about you. Everything that Jesus did and what the New Testament promises, is for you. There is nothing greater. It's the greatest thing that ever happened to you.

Romans 5:17 For if by one man's offence death reigned by one; much more they which receive abundance of grace and of the gift of righteousness shall reign in life by one, Jesus Christ.)

That sin that Adam committed brought spiritual death into the human race and it took another man, born of the Spirit of God, baptized with the Holy Spirit to reverse what happened there in THAT garden. Look at what Jests prayed in another garden – the Garden of Gethsemane on the night that He was arrested and brought in to be crucified:

Matthew 26:39 He went a little farther, and falling on His face, He prayed, "O My Father, if it is possible, let this cup pass from Me. Nevertheless, not as I will, but as You will." (MEV)

Jesus committed Himself to go through with it – He prayed that this task (or "cup") pass from Him "if it be possible". But it was not possible. The perfect man – the perfect sacrifice – God's only begotten Son was the only way the authority or power of death would be broken and the life of God would return to the spirit of man. There was no law or pattern of good works that people could perform to make it happen.

Galatians 3:21 Is the law then contrary to the promises of God? God forbid! For if there had been a law given which could have given life,

righteousness would indeed come through the law.
(MEV)

Right standing with God, or "salvation" could not come through a law. But it DID come. Jesus bought it for us.

Acts 4:12 Neither is there salvation in any other: for there is none other name under heaven given among men, whereby we must be saved.

There is no other Name by which we can be saved. In John 14:6, Jesus said that HE is the way the truth and the life and NO person will come to the Father but by Him. The greatest thing that ever happened to you, and all that it involves – every blessing that God provides, is in the perfect, finished work of Jesus Christ. The sin that separated us from God and the effect of that sin, i.e. poverty, sickness and spiritual death, were placed on Him – taken away by Him!

Isaiah 53:6 All of us like sheep have gone astray;
  each of us has turned to his own way,
but the LORD has laid on him
  the iniquity of us all.
(MEV)

So the things that separated us from God were placed on Him. Since He took them away, where does that leave you? You are brand new – a being that never existed before! Of course, if your hair is red when you are born again, your hair is still red. It's talking about the real you – the person on the inside – your spirit. Do you remember when Jesus was talking to Nicodemus in John 3? He talked about being born again. The spirit of man truly becomes born of God's Spirit – no longer separated from Him.

2 Corinthians 5:17 Therefore if any man be in Christ, he is a new creature: old things are passed away; behold, all things are become new.

The person on the inside becomes brand new!

18 And all things are of God, who hath reconciled us to himself by Jesus Christ, and hath given to us the ministry of reconciliation;
19 To wit, that God was in Christ, reconciling the world unto himself, not imputing their trespasses unto them; and hath committed unto us the word of reconciliation.
20 Now then we are ambassadors for Christ, as though God did beseech you by us: we pray you in Christ's stead, be ye reconciled to God.
21 For he hath made him to be sin for us, who knew no sin; that we might be made the righteousness of God in him.

This great passage of Scripture tells us of the extravagant gift of God. It summarizes the greatest thing that happened to you. You are a new creature. Your old life, your past, is not just over – it is GONE. All that need be done now is for the gift to be received. If people understand that God was in Christ, making the way for us to return to a family relationship with Him, they will know that it's theirs and they can have it by taking it. That's what the message is that we are to carry to the world: Here is Jesus – who He is and what He did and what it means to YOU. Remember the image of the serpent of brass, up on that pole? The symbol of Jesus on the cross? God made Jesus to be sin in our place so that in him, we become right with God. He became as we were so that we can become as He is. This is the greatest thing that ever happened to you! Look how verse 19 is stated in the Amplified Bible:

2 Corinthians 5:19 It was God [personally present] in Christ, reconciling *and* restoring the world to favor with Himself, not counting up *and* holding against [men] their trespasses [but cancelling them], and committing to us the message of reconciliation (of the restoration to favor).
(AMP)

It is a fact established in the court of Heaven that there is no sin held against you any longer. You are now able to accept the Father – child relationship that God offers and walk free – new and right with God. Any person, regardless of who you are or how you may have lived in the past, has presented to you the opportunity to have the life that God makes available. Prior to the coming of Jesus, the promised Messiah, it was only prophesied in Scripture, pointed to in the Law of

Moses but is now accomplished for you. THIS is the greatest thing that ever happened to you.

Here is the same passage of Scripture we just read, in The Living Bible paraphrase:

2 Corinthians 5:17-21 When someone becomes a Christian, he becomes a brand new person inside. He is not the same anymore. A new life has begun!

[18] All these new things are from God who brought us back to himself through what Christ Jesus did. And God has given us the privilege of urging everyone to come into his favor and be reconciled to him. [19] For God was in Christ, restoring the world to himself, no longer counting men's sins against them but blotting them out. This is the wonderful message he has given us to tell others. [20] We are Christ's ambassadors. God is using us to speak to you: we beg you, as though Christ himself were here pleading with you, receive the love he offers you—be reconciled to God. [21] For God took the sinless Christ and poured into him our sins. Then, in exchange, he poured God's goodness into us!

(TLB)

In the following chapters, we will explore knowing, having and living in the greatest thing that ever happened to you, through the greatest thing that God ever did, because of the greatest thing about Him!

Chapter 4
"Salvation"

Romans 10:13 For "whoever calls on the name of the Lord shall be saved."

In Christian terminology, we sometimes make being born again, receiving eternal life and being saved, seem synonymous. While they each describe right standing with God, or righteousness (right – ness) and having a Father – child relationship with him, they are not exactly the same thing. Several years ago, I met a young teenager who had been raised in a very nice but permissive home. His parents believed in God and believed that Christianity was "good" but they decided to not bring their children up in church or with any Godly instruction in the home. They wanted the child to "make up his own mind when the time comes". Well, that may be an enlightened sounding position but it is a sad way to abdicate the parental role in the most important part of a child's life. They might as well have said they wont teach their children to eat with silverware. They might as well say they wont teach their children to not play in traffic – they'll just know what to do when the time comes. While it's true that every person must accept Jesus for himself or herself, not telling children the truth about spiritual things is another way of saying they are just going to let the devil have their kids and hope everything turns out for the best.

I heard someone ask this young man if he had ever been saved. He replied, "From what?" As sad as his reply, it was very revealing in the sense that Christian people, people who are "saved", don't always grasp the "from what?" of salvation. We often think of it merely as saved from going to hell when you die. Mind you, if that WAS all it meant, it would be wonderful and well worth accepting and telling others about it. In His earthly ministry, Jesus spoke more about hell than he did about Heaven. They are both real. After leaving this world, everyone will spend eternity in one place or the other. God wants us to understand what actually happened to you because of the greatest thing He ever did. You will say, "Man oh man – this IS the greatest thing that ever happened to me."

We started this chapter with Romans 10:13. Whoever calls on the name of the Lord shall be "saved". In the language in which the book of Romans was written, the word saved is the Greek word sozo. This word means to save, deliver or protect (literally or figuratively) – heal, preserve, save (self), do well, be or make whole. Salvation was never just not going to hell. Religion re-invented the concept in order to keep people in bondage and make them less effective in the work of the Lord until they did leave here and make it to Heaven. Jesus not only removed sin from us. He removed the consequences of sin. I have heard some poor religious Christians say that the sicknesses and problems they suffer now are God's punishment for the way they lived before they were saved. Well, either Jesus paid for our sins or He didn't. If he did, let's walk in the fullness of what He provided. Believe me, if we are really going to accomplish what God wants us to do in the earth, we need to devour every morsel of truth about the finished work of Jesus in the plan of redemption. Take it – it's yours.

Colossians 1:13 He has delivered us from the power of darkness and has transferred us into the kingdom of His dear Son,
14 In whom we have redemption through His blood, the forgiveness of sins.
(MEV)

In describing salvation, these two verses tell us that God has delivered, or rescued us from the power of darkness. This word for power means authority, or the legal right to do something. What is darkness? It's descriptive of Satan, his kingdom, everything he has and everything he does. 2 Corinthians 6:14 says "What fellowship does light have with darkness?" there are two separate and distinct kingdoms. As part and parcel of our salvation, we have been delivered from the legal right for the devil or his kingdom to do anything to harm us, hinder us or resist God's blessing or our advancing Kingdom. He has transferred us into the Kingdom of God, RIGHT NOW! A kingdom is not a place. A kingdom is a government. People often think they will not get into the Kingdom of

God until they die. This says God HAS delivered us from the authority of darkness and HAS transferred us into the kingdom of God. Then why does it seem like the devil's allowed to do what he does? Because so many people don't understand salvation and what belongs to them. Ignorance and tradition keeps them in a soft little pew, sitting on their hands, hoping God will someday do something about what the devil's doing to them. Here's the big news – HE HAS ALREADY DONE IT! Jesus has all authority but until His Word and His Name are spoken into the situation by a member of His body (that's you and me – His church) that authority is not operating. Salvation IS NOT merely missing hell when you die. It's deliverance from the authority of hell while you're alive!

Then there's verse 14 which, speaking of Jesus, says that we have redemption through His Blood. That means we have been bought out of slavery. We have been redeemed from the curse in the earth because of sin. We are redeemed from the curse of the law.

Galatians 3:13 Christ hath redeemed us from the curse of the law, being made a curse for us: for it is written, Cursed is every one that hangeth on a tree:

14 That the blessing of Abraham might come on the Gentiles through Jesus Christ; that we might receive the promise of the Spirit through faith.

Notice the past tense of the word have: has or hath. Christ HAS redeemed us from the curse of the law. What's that? When God gave the law through Moses, God stated the blessing, or reward for keeping it and the punishment for breaking it. That punishment was called the curse of the law. Read Deuteronomy 28. Poverty, sickness and spiritual death, as well as failure, depression and fear, are in the curse of the law – THAT is what you have been redeemed from NOW. Not when you get to Heaven. You wont need redemption from these things in Heaven. There is none of that up there. If redemption isn't till the next life, what makes people think the curse is for this life? No – by hanging on that tree, Christ redeemed us from the curse of the law so that the blessing can come on us through faith!

Ephesians 1:3 Blessed *be* the God and Father of our Lord Jesus Christ, who has blessed us with every spiritual blessing in the heavenly *places* in Christ,
(NKJV)

In this new Kingdom of which we are members, we have every spiritual blessing. That doesn't just refer to happy feelings and future enjoyment – everything that happens in this physical world starts in the spiritual realm. Remember the act of creation we discussed in Chapter 1. Everything you need has already been credited to your account because it belongs to Jesus and you are in Him.

Look back at Colossians 1:14. The word "forgiveness" of sins doesn't just mean kind tolerance and God saying, "Oh honey, it's okay – I know you didn't mean to." It means remission. Remission is an accounting term that means the bill held against us has been paid and the account has been cleared. In the database of Heaven, the sin ledger shows that you have a zero balance. The Blood of Jesus is the delete button on that Heavenly computer.

Galatians 1:4 who gave Himself for our sins, that He might deliver us from this present evil age, according to the will of our God and Father,
(NKJV)

Jesus has NOW delivered us from the power of darkness and redeemed us from the curse of the law. We are delivered from this present evil age. We haven't physically left here – it means we are delivered from the power and authority of this evil world system, over which Satan is god (2 Corinthians 4:4). That includes the Old Testament pronouncements of visiting the iniquity of the fathers on the children and great grandchildren and so on. We have been entirely redeemed from the entire curse of the entire law. The entire blessing is now entirely ours. The passages we read in Galatians and Colossians show that salvation is not just avoiding hell when we die. It's more than just rescue in this life, out of darkness and the curse. They show us that we have been brought into the

Kingdom of God with all its authority, power and blessing. Salvation enables us to be free from the grasp of the devil and authorizes us use the Word of God and the Name of Jesus to do the works in the earth that we are called to do until Jesus returns!

Chapter 5
"The Grace of God"

Ephesians 2:8 For by grace you have been saved through faith, and that not of yourselves; *it is* the gift of God,
9 not of works, lest anyone should boast.
10 For we are His workmanship, created in Christ Jesus for good works, which God prepared beforehand that we should walk in them.
(NKJV)

This passage of Scripture summarizes all we have discussed to this point. The greatest thing about God is that He is Love. The greatest expression of love has produced the greatest thing that ever happened to us. We are saved by grace. NOT by works, lest any person should think they earned it. We are re-created. We are creatures that never before existed and the character of this new creation has all the blessings of God and the nature of God to use these blessings to help others.

Grace is a topic that has lately received a lot of attention. Grace cannot be discussed too much. We are better off discussing it a lot than too little. However it can be incorrectly defined and misunderstood. I want to explain it simply because it is a simple concept. In fact, everything in the Bible is simple. It's just spiritual. Religious tradition and deception try to tangle it up like a bird's nest in our minds. But it is simple. Let's trust the Teacher of the church, the Holy Spirit, to help us to understand it spiritually.

Here are a couple of common statements about grace. As an acronym, it's G.od's R.iches A.t C.hrist's E.xpense. That's what it's about alright. It is called unmerited favor. That it is. It is called God's willingness to treat us as though sin never existed. That's the heart of it. Grace is not a New Testament policy that makes sin acceptable. Grace is not a substitute for faith, for we are not saved by grace alone. We are saved by grace through faith. Ephesians 2:10 goes on to say that we are God's workmanship, created in Christ unto good works. Not to earn our position with Him, but because we are now like Him! The blessing and forgiving side of grace is only part of it. Just as love has two expressions, mercy and compassion, grace is divine favor working for us and divine influence working in us. Grace draws us to God and influences us.

1 Corinthians 15:10 But what I am I am by the grace of God., and His grace bestowed upon me did not prove ineffectual. But I labored more strenuously than all the rest – yet it was not I, but God's grace working with me.
(Weymouth)

Grace is God reaching. Just as faith is the hand that reaches out to God, grace is God's hand reaching out to us. 1 Corinthians 13 says though I have all faith to move mountains, without love I am nothing. My faith could reach out to God for the rest of my life but without His grace, there would be nothing there for me. The acronym I use for grace is; "G.od R.eaching A.nd C.hrist E.mpowering". Grace is His hand reaching out to me, receiving me, healing me, helping me, blessing me, supplying me, equipping me and empowering me. What does grace provide? Everything.

Galatians 2:20 I am crucified with Christ: nevertheless I live; yet not I, but Christ liveth in me: and the life which I now live in the flesh I live by the faith of the Son of God, who loved me, and gave himself for me.

21 I do not frustrate the grace of God: for if righteousness come by the law, then Christ is dead in vain.

This is very simple. What Jesus did, He did for us. God put our lost condition on Jesus so that we could have His right standing with the Father. So I am crucified with Christ. I am not, as religious tradition says, "just a sinner saved by grace". I WAS a sinner. I got saved by grace through faith and NOW I live this new life, as a new creature in Christ! I was on that tree, IN HIM. Yet I live, by the power of God that His gift provides me. If my righteousness or right standing comes by my own performance, Christ didn't need to die. Don't you remember when we read that if there had been a law that could make us right with God, just as Jesus prayed in the garden, the cup would have passed from Him? We wouldn't need His sacrifice.

Then the Scripture here goes on to say Paul doesn't frustrate the grace of God. If grace is the hand of God reaching to us (and through us), how can you frustrate it? Suppose you and I were out on the ocean in a boat and I fell overboard. You stop the boat alongside me and I'm there in the water flailing away. What if when you reach out to me, I wont stop flailing and reach back? I'm going to drown and your effort to save me will be frustrated. That's how we frustrate the grace of God. He reaches out to us and we wont reach back because we think "I got this." That's what it means to be not under the law but under grace:

Romans 6:12 Let not sin therefore reign in your mortal body, that ye should obey it in the lusts thereof.

13 Neither yield ye your members as instruments of unrighteousness unto sin: but yield yourselves unto God, as those that are alive from the dead, and your members as instruments of righteousness unto God.

14 For sin shall not have dominion over you: for ye are not under the law, but under grace.

15 What then? shall we sin, because we are not under the law, but under grace? God forbid.

16 Know ye not, that to whom ye yield yourselves servants to obey, his servants ye are to whom ye obey; whether of sin unto death, or of obedience unto righteousness?

We are not under law but under grace. This means we are not under the law of works. We don't have to earn what we need from God. It's given to you free of charge to you. What does grace provide? Remission of sin, right standing with God, power to live free from sin and everything else we need. Everything.

I enjoy watching tennis. Every time I watch a tennis tournament on television, I am awed by the way the players move around the court. They are so graceful. Even the most muscular male player has a graceful way of moving side to side and running toward the baseline to get to the ball. To me, they are like ballet dancers with tennis racquets. Graceful. Even though you realize that it's difficult work that only a few people in the world can do with that level of skill, it looks effortless. That's why it's graceful. By the grace of God, we can do that which is not possible *by our effort*. Grace is doing the impossible by God's effort working through us. In 2 Corinthians 12:9, when God told the Apostle Paul "My grace is sufficient for you", He told him, "You will overcome this 'thorn' – this spiritual opposition, by MY effort. Not yours. So Paul learned to glory in his own weakness because he knew that when he relied on God and not himself, God's effort would bring him through to victory. Being not under law but under grace means we are no longer "working to appease God" but "resting in God who works in us and through us. He reaches toward us and we take hold by our faith in Him. The life of a believer is graceful. The grace of God removes emphasis from effort on our part to the finished work on HIS part.

His hand reaches toward a lost and dying world but they are all too often reaching in another direction. I know many morally good people who think they're right with God because they don't kill people or rob banks. Some people think they are right with God because they support social justice and political correctness. I know Christians who receive the new birth experience but are living with heavy burdens, thinking they have to earn the very things that God has already given them. They don't avail themselves of these things because they are reaching to their own effort to attain it rather than reaching by faith in God to receive it. There is no other way to receive salvation (and we have just looked at how far reaching and wonderful salvation is) but by grace through faith.

When we read the story of the Prodigal Son, we often just look at how the father welcomed the son who returned. We also then look at the reaction of the other son when their father celebrated the prodigal's return. Look at the astonishing statement the father made to the son who didn't leave:

Luke 15:31 "And he said to him, 'Son, you are always with me, and all that I have is yours.
(NKJV)

This is your place with your Heavenly Father right now. You don't have to die to receive this. This is your position NOW. You are always with Him and all that He has is yours. You are all He has made you. You have all He has given you. You can do all He has planned for you. THAT, my brother or sister, is grace.

Chapter 6
"Faith Receives"

Romans 5:1 Therefore being justified by faith, we have peace with God through our Lord Jesus Christ:
2 By whom also we have access by faith into this grace wherein we stand, and rejoice in hope of the glory of God.

We began the last chapter with the statement that we are saved by grace through faith. Throughout Scripture, we see the grace of God extended time and time again. The ones who applied faith, got it. The Hebrew children were the recipients of great mercy and grace from God but a whole generation died in the wilderness because God's promise did them no good. Why? They didn't mix faith with it.

Hebrews 4:2 For unto us was the gospel preached, as well as unto them: but the word preached did not profit them, not being mixed with faith in them that heard it.

This is talking about the very people who were led out of Egypt and were told to go take the Promised Land. Could they have taken the land? Of course. But they didn't. Why? They didn't believe what God told them. That land was promised. It was theirs, yet they died in the wilderness, never having received it. So often we hear people say that if God wants such and such for me, why it doesn't happen? The promise, standing alone never has produced the intended result in a person's life. The Hebrews who believed the promise went in. They had to wait for the unbelievers to pass away but they still got it. Verse 2 of Romans 5 says that it's by faith that we have access to the grace of God. The grace of God is here. The promises are true. Without faith, there is no access to that grace. No amount of emphasis on grace will ever substitute for faith. Everything God has for us – from the new birth to our heavenly home and every blessing in between and beyond, is by the grace of God but unless we apply faith, we can't have it.

What is faith?

Hebrews 11:1 Now faith is the substance of things hoped for, the evidence of things not seen.

Grace provides it. God's Word says it. Hope wants it. Faith takes it. Faith is the spiritual substance of what we hope for, or what we want to have or happen. It is THE evidence of the thing that exists in the spiritual realm – remember, the blessing of God starts there. Faith goes into the spirit realm and pulls it into the material world. It's our hand that grasps the hand of God's grace.

How does faith come?

Romans 10:17 So then faith cometh by hearing, and hearing by the word of God.

Faith for what you need comes by hearing what God says about it. It doesn't come by having heard. You must feed your faith. Don't be like people one minister described, feeding your body three hot meals a day and your spirit one cold snack a week. Faith begins where the will of God is known. You cannot know God's will for you by listening to religious people rationalize why their cousin didn't get it. Remember, in the courtroom of your mind, the evidence that will win is faith in God. If your mind chooses the evidence of feelings or circumstances, the circumstance will win.

Where is faith and how does it work?

Romans 10:8 But what saith it? The word is nigh thee, even in thy mouth, and in thy heart: that is, the word of faith, which we preach;

9 That if thou shalt confess with thy mouth the Lord Jesus, and shalt believe in thine heart that God hath raised him from the dead, thou shalt be saved.

10 For with the heart man believeth unto righteousness; and with the mouth confession is made unto salvation.

Don't forget what we learned about salvation. It's not just going to Heaven when we leave this world. It is salvation, deliverance, healing and wholeness. It is the totality of our deliverance from the power of darkness and our redemption from the curse of the law. Here is the Word of faith which we preach: confess with your mouth and believe in your heart. With the heart you believe. You receive what God says before you ever see it. Then with your mouth you confess and keep it confessed till you see it. Faith is in your heart. It is not in your head or your body. Believing is not feeling. It is not wishing. It's not will power. It is accepting in your heart, the evidence of what God said about it over the outside evidence or what you see or feel. Don't be moved by what you see or feel. Be moved only by what you believe. Then you say it.

"That sounds like name – it – and – claim – it." Well, my answer is that this whole thing – your life and all you will ever see or do, is all about Jesus Christ - who He is and what He did. God the Father named Him and I claimed Him. From the instant of creation, we see the application of faith in the use of words. It worked over and over in the lives of the Old Testament followers of God. It worked in the life and ministry of Jesus. He told us that this is how faith works. If you think that faith is just something you have and that people who receive the blessings just have more and others have less, you're going contrary to what Jesus Himself said to do. A small amount of faith, applied the way Jesus said to do it, produces great results.

Luke 17:6 And the Lord said, If ye had faith as a grain of mustard seed, ye might say unto this sycamine tree, Be thou plucked up by the root, and be thou planted in the sea; and it should obey you.

If you have the faith but don't ever apply it by saying, that sycamine tree isn't going to move. That sycamine tree represents what needs to be changed in your life. You received the new birth by grace through faith, when you believed and said. You confessed that Jesus is Lord and believed in your heart that God raised Him from the dead. Why expect this to be one kind of faith but when it comes to everything else, it works differently? It works exactly the same way. Jesus said so. Don't argue in your mind over who tried it or did it wrong or who said they had ten million dollars and didn't have it. Look at God's Word. If you believe it, say it and do it, it will work. If you don't, you can never again say it didn't happen because it just wasn't God's will. You know better. The same faith that got you born again is the same faith you live by. Don't quit because you don't see things change instantly. Hope sees what God has provided by His grace. Faith reaches into the spirit realm and grasps the hand of God and brings it into the natural.

Galatians 3:11b The just shall live by faith.

The greatest thing that God ever did was the redemption of mankind through the finished work of Jesus Christ. The greatest thing that ever happened to you is this full redemption provided by the outstretched hand of God's grace, received by your hand of faith. There is nothing you will ever need, no problem you will ever face, no assignment you will ever receive from God that this salvation by grace, does not provide more than enough supply to meet every need and make you victorious. Choose to believe it, say it and act on it.

Chapter 7
"Your Most Important Decisions"

If you have read to this point and still not availed yourself of the greatest thing that ever happened to you, you need to do so right now. The free gift of salvation and all that it entails, and all that God provided through the finished work of Jesus Christ, is available to you. Here is what to do next:

Romans 3:23 For all have sinned, and come short of the glory of God;

Everyone has sinned. Nobody is yet perfect. Even the most moral person you ever met, at some point, has sinned. This is the condition of the world. Without Jesus Christ, the world is without hope.

Romans 6:23 For the wages of sin *is* death; but the gift of God *is* eternal life through Jesus Christ our Lord.

As you just read, sin separated us from God. But God didn't leave us in this condition. Thank God, through Jesus, you are now offered the gift of eternal life. Regardless of your accomplishments, if you are without Jesus Christ as your own Savior, you are without hope, without God in this world. But no matter what you're facing, you CAN have this He has already made the way for you to be born again and brought into the Kingdom of God. Make the decision to accept God's free gift of eternal life. It is your MOST important decision!

Romans 10:9 That if thou shalt confess with thy mouth the Lord Jesus, and shalt believe in thine heart that God hath raised him from the dead, thou shalt be saved.

10 For with the heart man believeth unto righteousness; and with the mouth confession is made unto salvation.

Jesus Christ loves you so much that He left His Heavenly home, came to earth, and died for you, just as if you were the only person on earth. Everything He did, He did for YOU. God wants to make you his very own Child and it is His desire to bless your life with His power!

Ephesians 2:8 For by grace are ye saved through faith; and that not of yourselves: *it is* the gift of God:

Here's how to receive the free gift of eternal life:

Pray this prayer:

"Jesus, I believe you died for me. I believe God raised you from the dead. I confess you as my Lord and receive for myself, the gift of eternal life. I repent of sin and turn to you. I renounce the devil and everything he stands for. I belong to you, Jesus. Come into my heart. Wash me with your Blood and make me a new creature. Thank you for saving me, Lord. I am now born again and saved by your grace through faith. In Jesus' Name, Amen."

If you prayed that prayer, you have received God's greatest gift.

II Corinthians 5: 17 Therefore if any man *be* **in Christ,** *he is* **a new creature: old things are passed away; behold, all things are become new.**

You are now a new creature – you have been made brand new inside! You are God's very own child and a member of the church, which is His body. Contact a Bible believing Church and tell someone today that Jesus is your Lord!

Receiving the Baptism in the Holy Spirit"

Acts 1:8 But ye shall receive power, after that the Holy Ghost is come upon you: and ye shall be witnesses unto me both in Jerusalem, and in all Judaea, and in Samaria, and unto the uttermost part of the earth.

Now let's talk about receiving a gift that is separate from the new birth, which is the baptism with the Holy Spirit. Remember that it is also a free gift. It does not have to be earned to be received. You are not required to feel "good enough" or "holy enough." I once heard the testimony of a woman who told her pastor that she now realized that the Baptism in the Holy Spirit is real and that is was for her. The pastor offered to pray with her to receive. Then she said, "No, not yet. I still have some more cleaning up to do before I'm ready." Her pastor said, "Let me ask you something. Now, I know that you're saved. You're a born again Christian. If you died right now, would you go to Heaven?" The woman said, "Yes, of course." "Well," the Pastor replied, "If you're ready to go to Heaven, you're ready to get a little more Heaven in you!" The man Saul, later Apostle Paul, was topped by the Lord and saved on the road to Damascus. The next thing he knew, here came Ananias to help him get the Holy Ghost! IF Saul had gotten to Damascus and not been stopped by Jesus Himself, he was going to arrest Christians.

The Holy Spirit gets to work on you, don't worry about that. But God is Love. He is the most gentle and sweet instructor that you could imagine. You could have hands laid on you to receive the Baptism in the Holy Spirit. But you don't have to. My Grandmother, who was baptized n the Holy Ghost, like I said before, often told me that this Baptism in the Holy Spirit was something that I desperately needed. However, she never told me how to go about receiving it. You see, she "tarried" and waited for an emotional experience to trigger her receiving. Some people still do it. They go to church and kneel at the altar for hours, years on end, begging and pleading for God to let them have the Holy Spirit

Luke 11:11 If a son shall ask bread of any of you that is a father, will he give him a stone? or if he ask a fish, will he for a fish give him a serpent?

12 Or if he shall ask an egg, will he offer him a scorpion?

13 If ye then, being evil, know how to give good gifts unto your children: how much more shall your heavenly Father give the Holy Spirit to them that ask him?

You don't have to use my words, but ask God to baptize you in the Holy Spirit. Tell Him that you want to receive the baptism in the Holy Spirit and to speak, pray, and sing in other tongues.

Then receive it by faith. Know that it is God's will for you.

I John 5:14 And this is the confidence that we have in him, that, if we ask any thing according to his will, he heareth us.

15 And if we know that he hears us, whatsoever we ask, we know that we have the petitions that we desired of him.

This may sound like I'm trying to make it too easy but it is just this simple. All you have to do is desire it, ask for it, and take it. To be honest with you, this is how you receive anything (I mean anything) that God promises you in the Bible. Someone asked, "Well if God wants us to have 'this and that,' why does it seem like He makes it so hard?" God doesn't make it complicated. We are the ones who make it complicated by opinions, reasoning and doubt

James 1:6 But let him ask in faith, nothing wavering. For he that wavereth is like a wave of the sea driven with the wind and tossed.

7 For let not that man think that he shall receive anything of the Lord.

Asking in faith isn't hard. Remember, just desire it, ask for it, and take it. You desire the Baptism in the Holy Spirit. You desire the power of God in your life. You desire the gifts of the Spirit, including your own supernatural prayer language. You will speak in tongues. You know that it is God's will to give it to you. Now just ask for it. "Taking it" is where your faith comes in. If you're born again, you have all the faith it takes. You already believed for the New Birth – taking something spiritually dead and making it spiritually alive. I know you have enough faith to receive the Baptism in the Holy Ghost. Just take it! You have it!

Then just relax and start talking. Say the words that you don't understand. Don't worry if it doesn't sound like a language to you – but it will be your "prayer language. You can't each someone to speak in tongues. You don't need to. But as you begin, just start talking. The Holy Spirit gives you the utterance. Now, just like a baby when he first begins to talk, the more you do it, the more fluent you will become. It will flow. Just keep it up. You don't need to worry about getting an interpretation for this. Remember – there are "various kinds of tongues." This is the "kind" that is personal, rather than a message to the congregation. Here is something that will help you receive.

Luke 12:11And when they bring you unto the synagogues, and unto magistrates, and powers, take ye no thought how or what thing ye shall answer, or what ye shall say:
12 For the Holy Ghost shall teach you in the same hour what ye ought to say.

This verse is not about receiving the baptism with the Holy Spirit with the Biblical evidence of speaking in tongues but the principle is similar. The Holy Spirit gives you what to say but you have to say it. Remember what happened to Peter, the man who denied Jesus three times on the night of Jesus' arrest. On the Day of Pentecost he preached by the power of the Holy Spirit and three thousand souls were added to the Kingdom of God! Steven, a deacon who in Acts Chapter 7, preached the history of the Jewish faith and connected it to the New Covenant, showing that Jesus is the Christ. We think of the men in the Book of Acts as mighty men of God and so they were but it was the Holy Spirit in them that made them mighty. He shows us where to go but we have to do the going. He honors our faith and does the doing. If you will step out and put the air across your vocal chords and begin to speak words you don't understand, just as the 120 on the Day of Pentecost, just as the believers in Samaria, Ephesus and the house of Cornelius – just as the Apostle Paul, the Holy Spirit will honor your faith and give you supernatural utterance.

"Lord Jesus, I trust in you. I know I'm saved. I see in the Word of God that you want me to have the power to do the works that You did and greater works. I have received you as Savior and Lord. Now I also receive You as my Baptizer in the Holy Spirit. You said that you would give me the Baptism in the Holy Spirit if I ask for it. I'm asking. I make love my aim and I desire to be used by You according to Your will. So I ask you now to baptize me in the Holy Spirit, in the Name of Jesus. I now receive it by faith, in Jesus' Name.

I thank you for it and I thank you for my supernatural prayer language which I now enjoy."

Now, begin speaking the words the Holy Spirit gives you and be blessed by the fullness of God's presence in your life!

OTHER BOOKS BY DAVID M. GILLESPIE

"Have You Received the Holy Spirit?"

"The Gift of Righteousness"

"Faith Worketh by Love"

"Patience"

"Content but Not Satisfied"

"Two Kinds of Sovereignty"

"The Eyes of Your Understanding"

"In Him Scriptures"

"Healing Scriptures"

"Concerning Spiritual Gifts"

"Letters from Luke"

http://amazon.com/author/davidmgillespie

Made in the USA
Columbia, SC
15 March 2022

57490954R00035